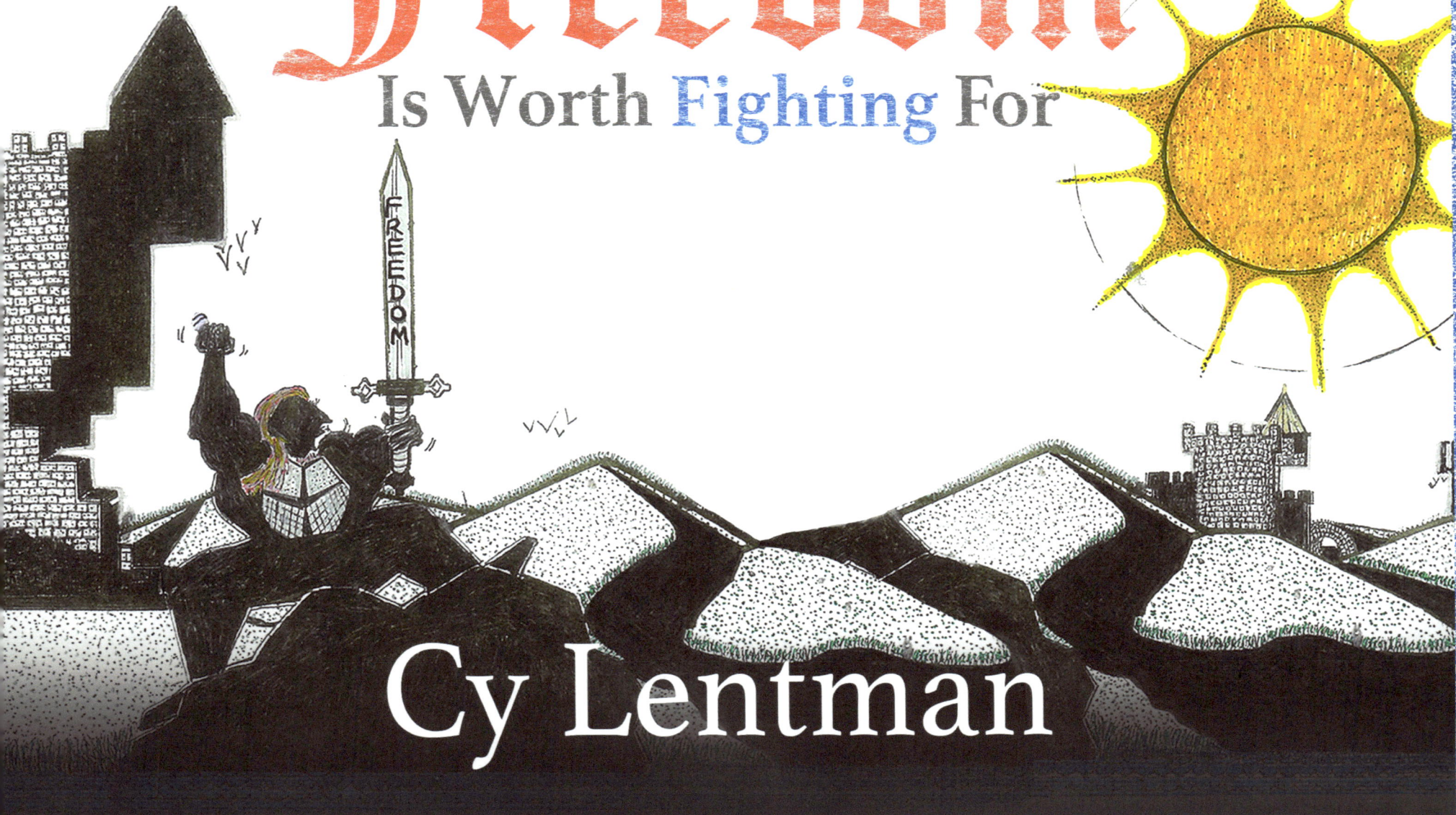

SEIZE THE DAY

Freedom

Is Worth Fighting For

Cy Lentman

ISBN: 978-1-64704-493-0 (hardcover)
ISBN: 978-1-64704-492-3 (eBook)

Dedicated to my mother, Katherine—
my inspiration and my confidant.

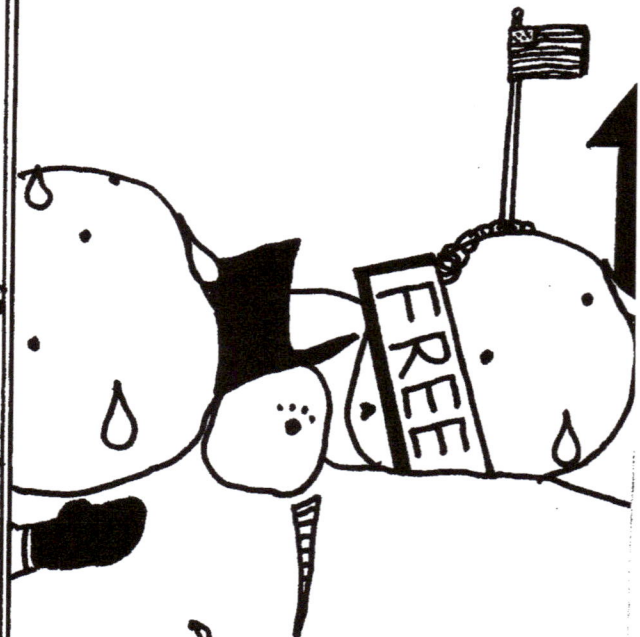

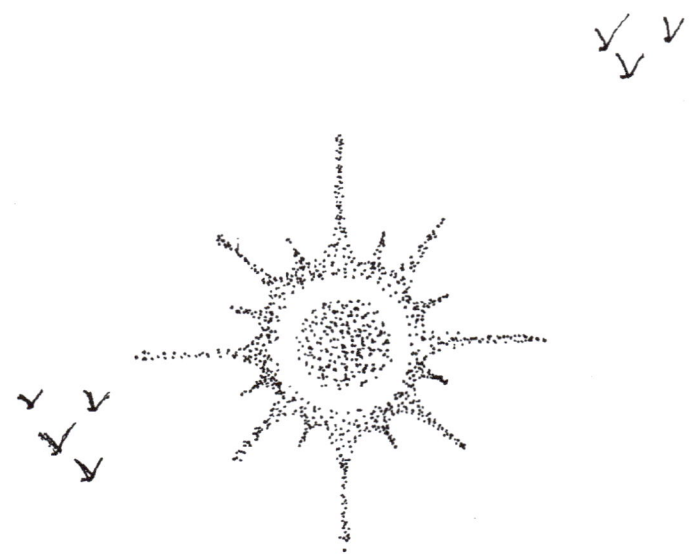

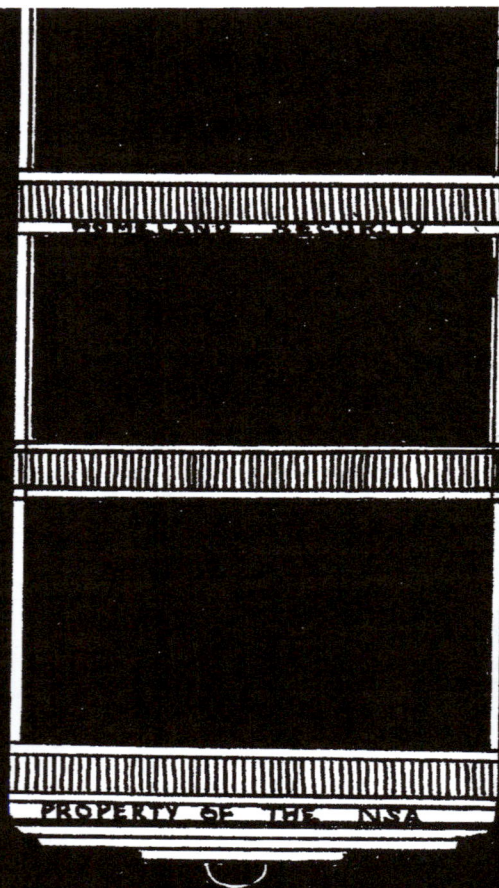

CARPE
COFFEE
DIEᴹ HARD.

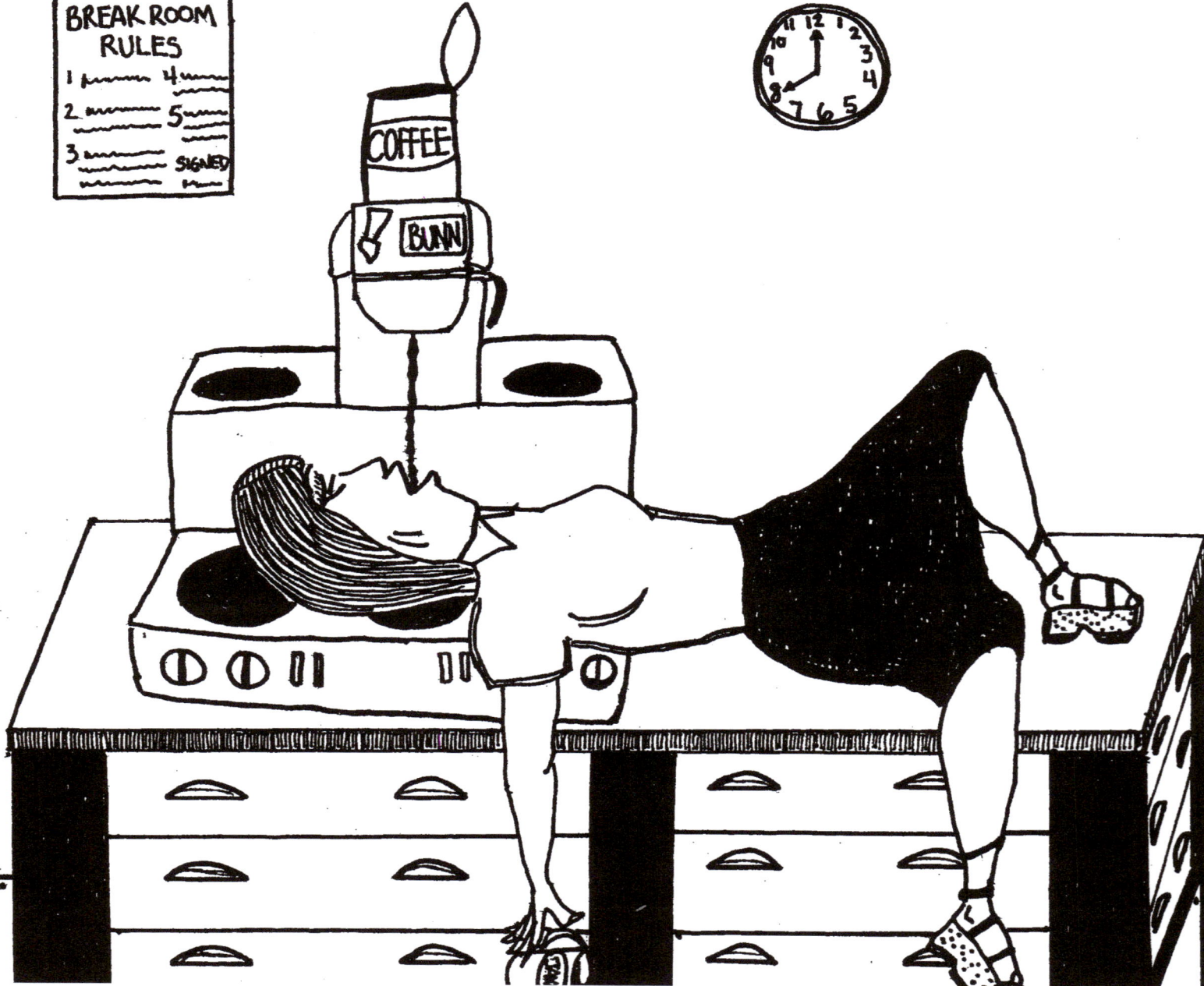

THE COFFEE TROUGH CAFE

OPEN 6-9
WHERE
IOWA
MEETS
MANHATTAN

FRESH COFFEE

FRESH COFFEE

© DUSSEAU '08
1/28

SALE

SALE

SEASONS GREEDY

QUARTZ

© DUSSEAU '18

MORTGAGE DEPARTMENT
WE CATER TO ECONOMIC DISPARITY

WATER FOUNTAIN

ALTERNATE METHODS OF PAYMENT

© DUSSEAU '07

MOTEL

NO VACANCY

RICH

MUNICIPAL
PARK

NO VAGRANCY

© DUSSEAU '07

BOTTLE RETURN

ATM

BANK

DUSSEAU

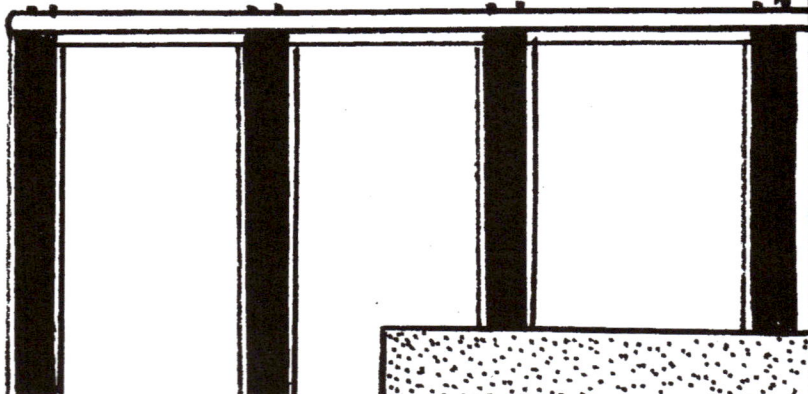

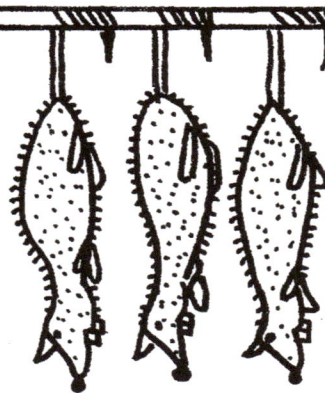

DONNA (HANGOVER) HANOVER

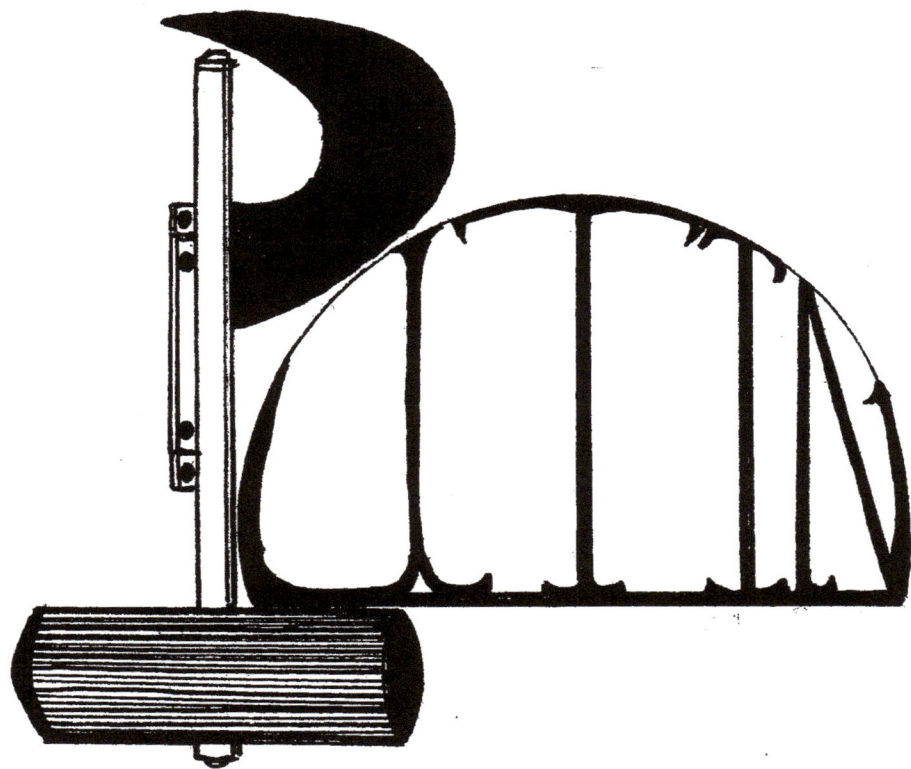

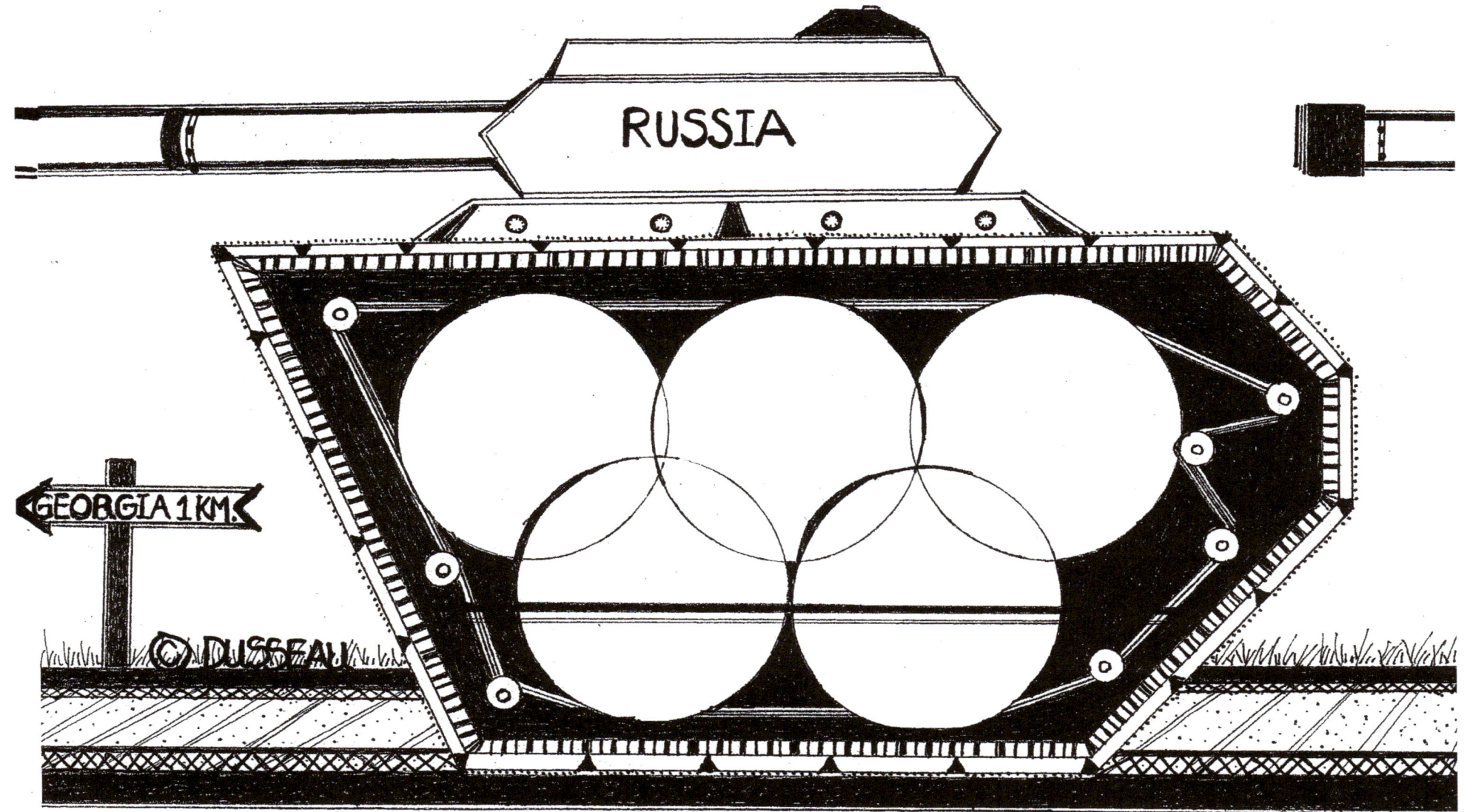

CAPTURING THE OLYMPIC SPIRIT.

RUSSIA

GEORGIA 1 KM.

© DUSSEAU

THE POWER OF MEDIA.

THE NEW YORK TIMES

© DUSSEAU '08 2/22

POLITICAL CLIMATE CHANGE

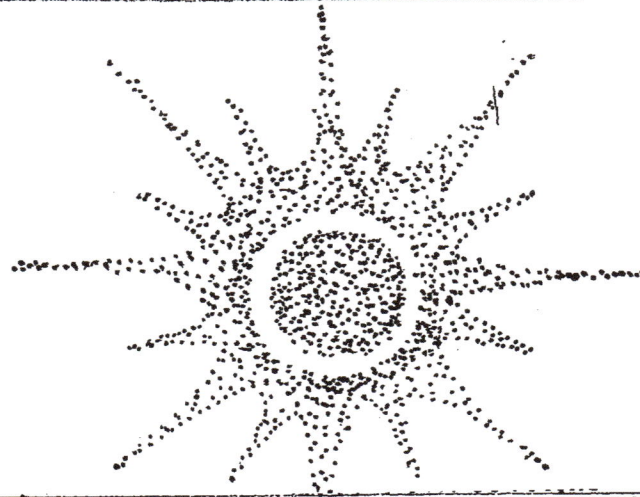

RETIREMENT

THE ELDERLY

SOCIAL SECURITY

MEDICARE

THE MUSEUM OF EXTINCT SPECIES

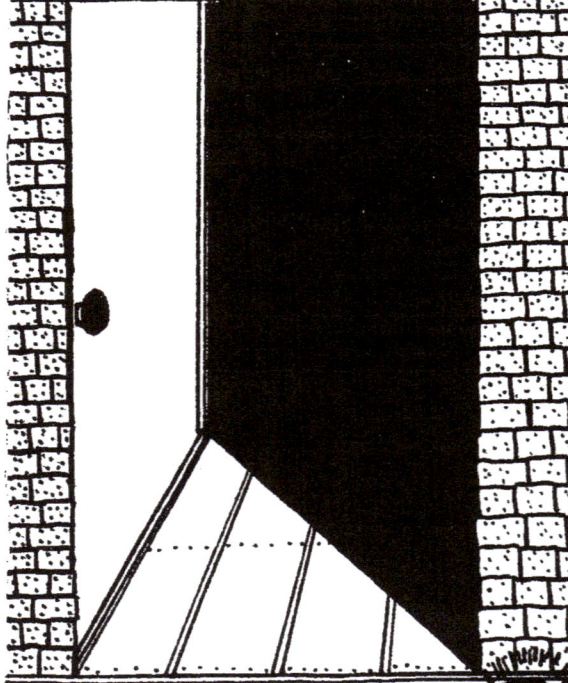

THE MIDDLE CLASS

THE MILKMAN

© DUSSEAU '08
2/8

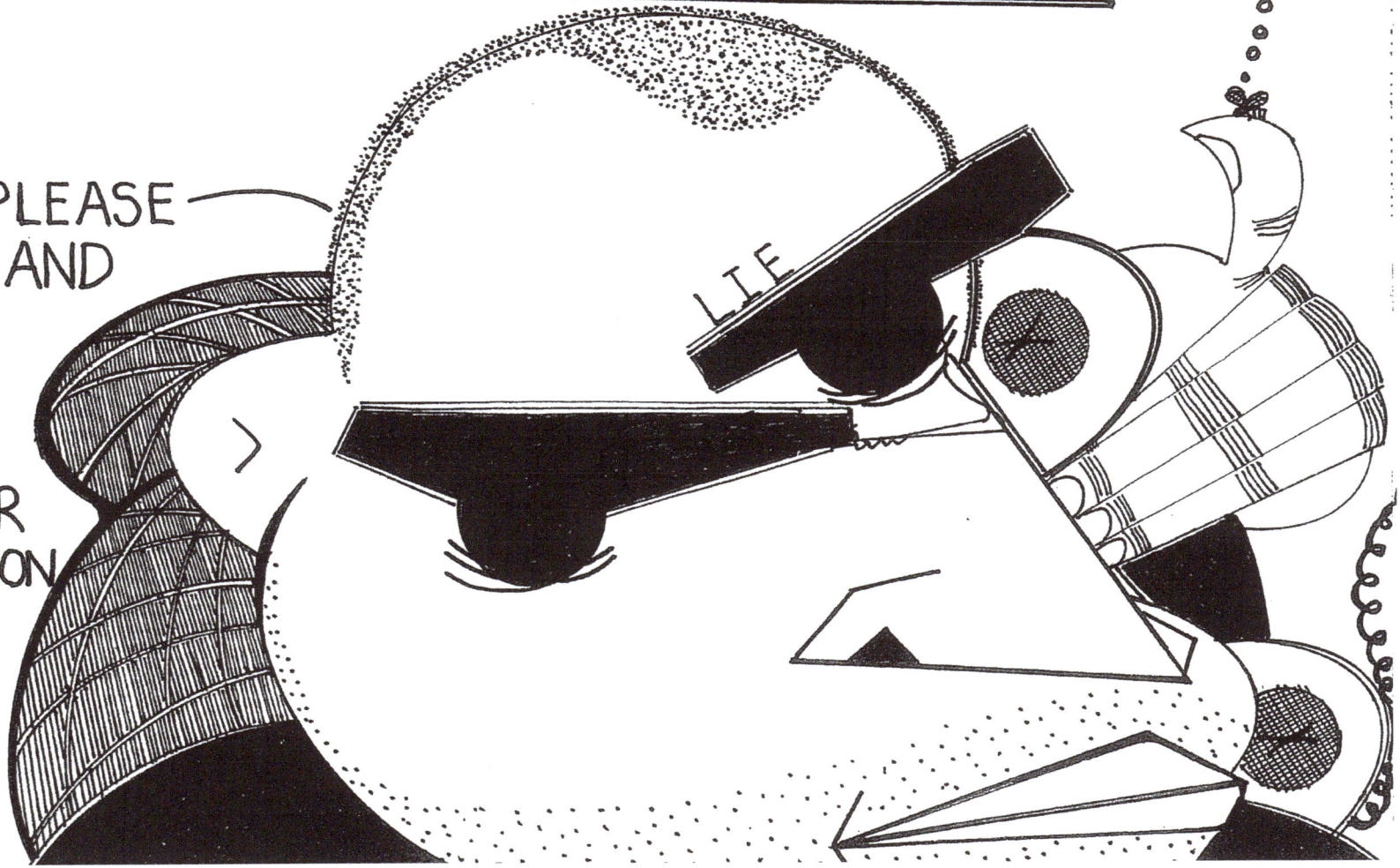

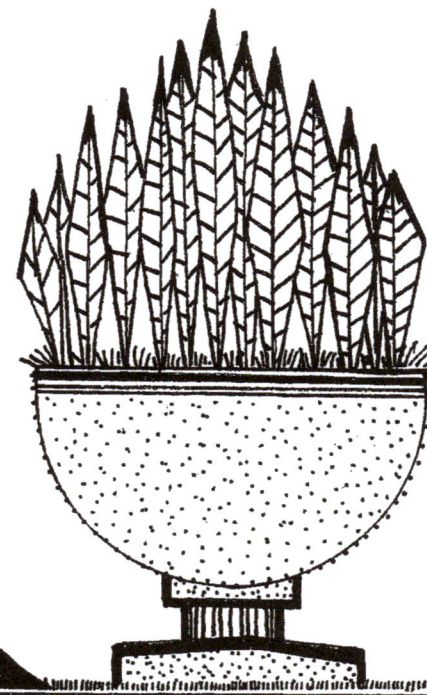

SAN ANTONIO, TEXAS: SO AS NOT TO OFFEND MEXICAN-AMERICANS IN THIS COUNTRY, OBAMA HAS THE ALAMO REPLACED WITH A STATUE OF GOODWILL.

CORONA

© DUSSEAU '14

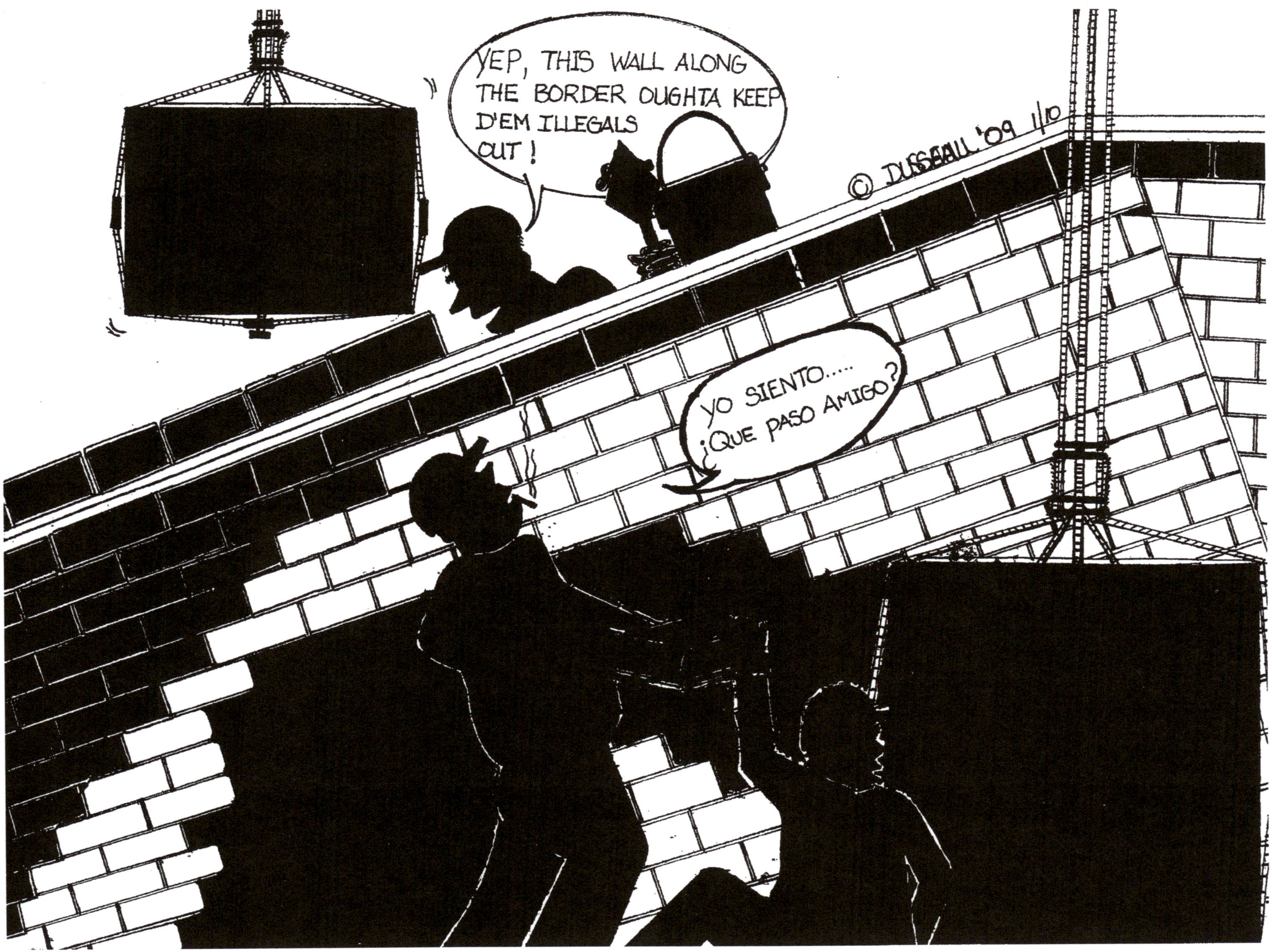

U.S. NAT'L DEBT

© DUSSEAU

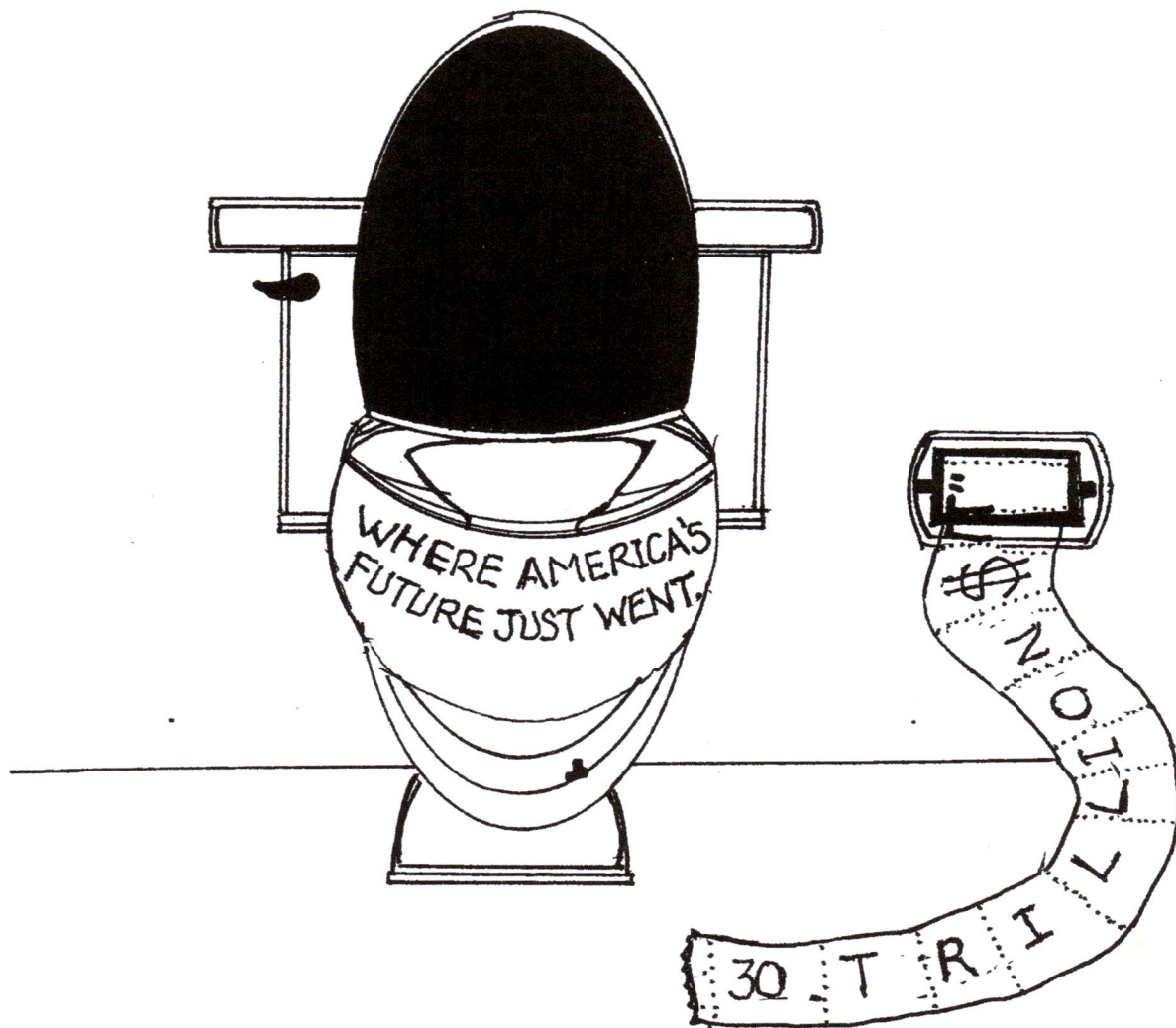

GLO-BEAR WARMING.

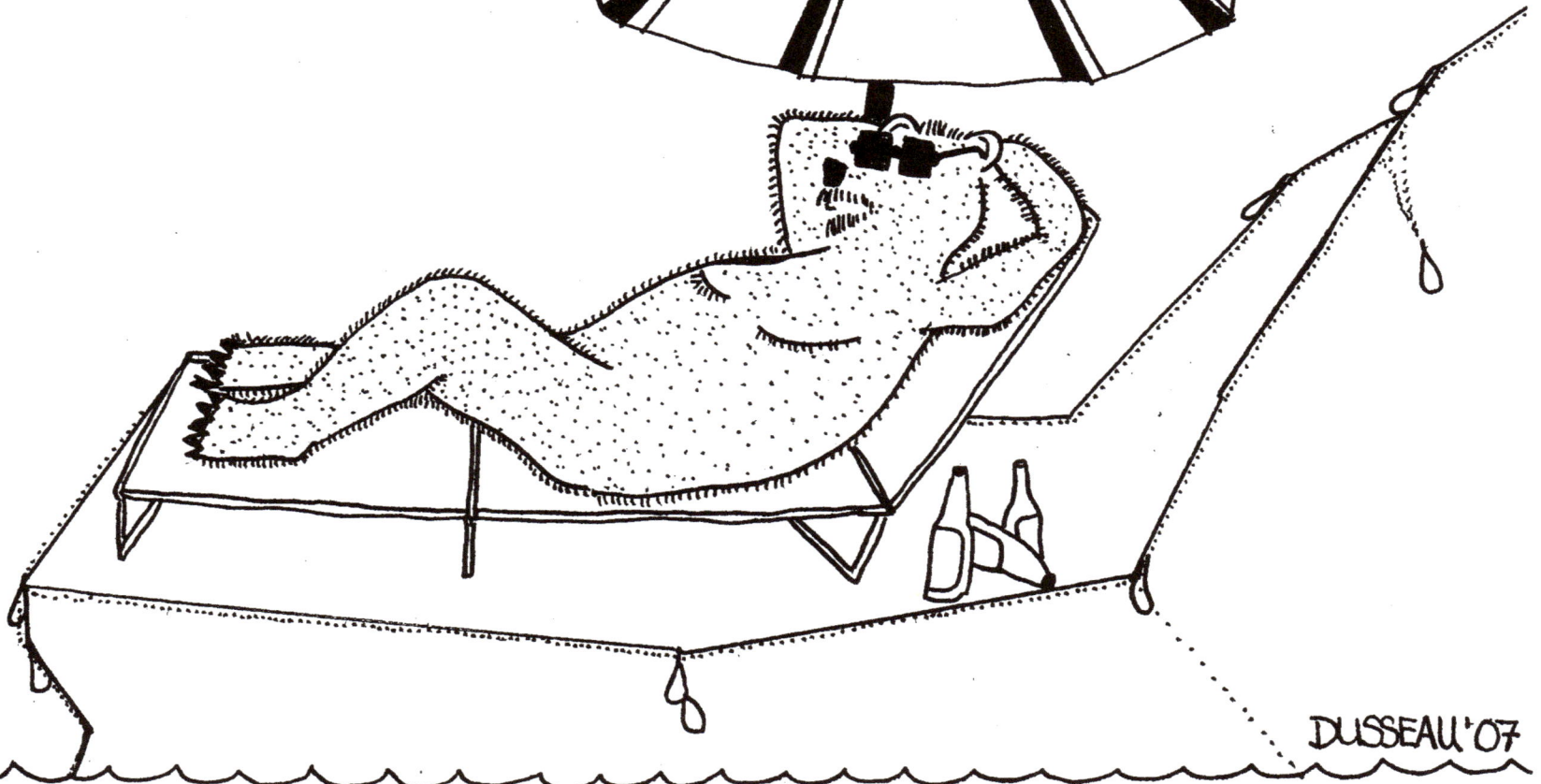

DUSSEAU '07

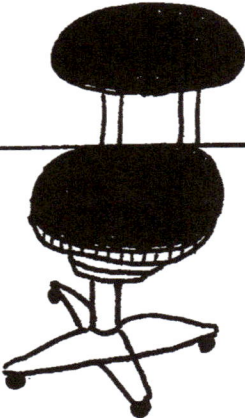

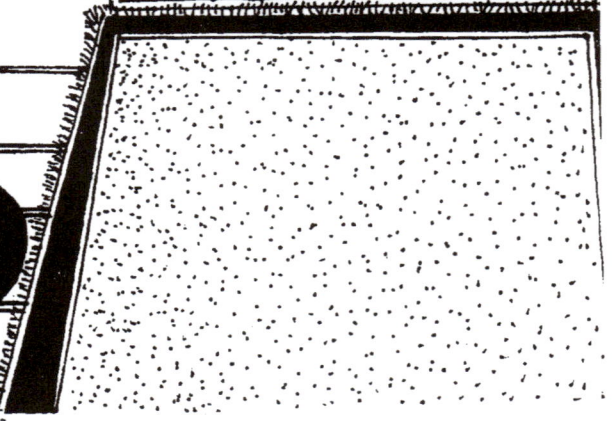

BRITNEY SPHERES

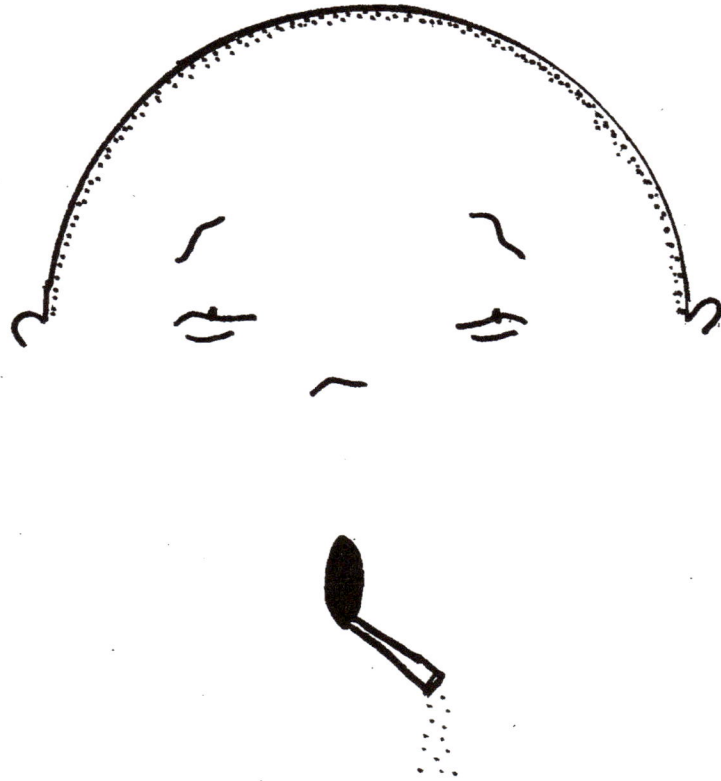

© DUSSEAU 07

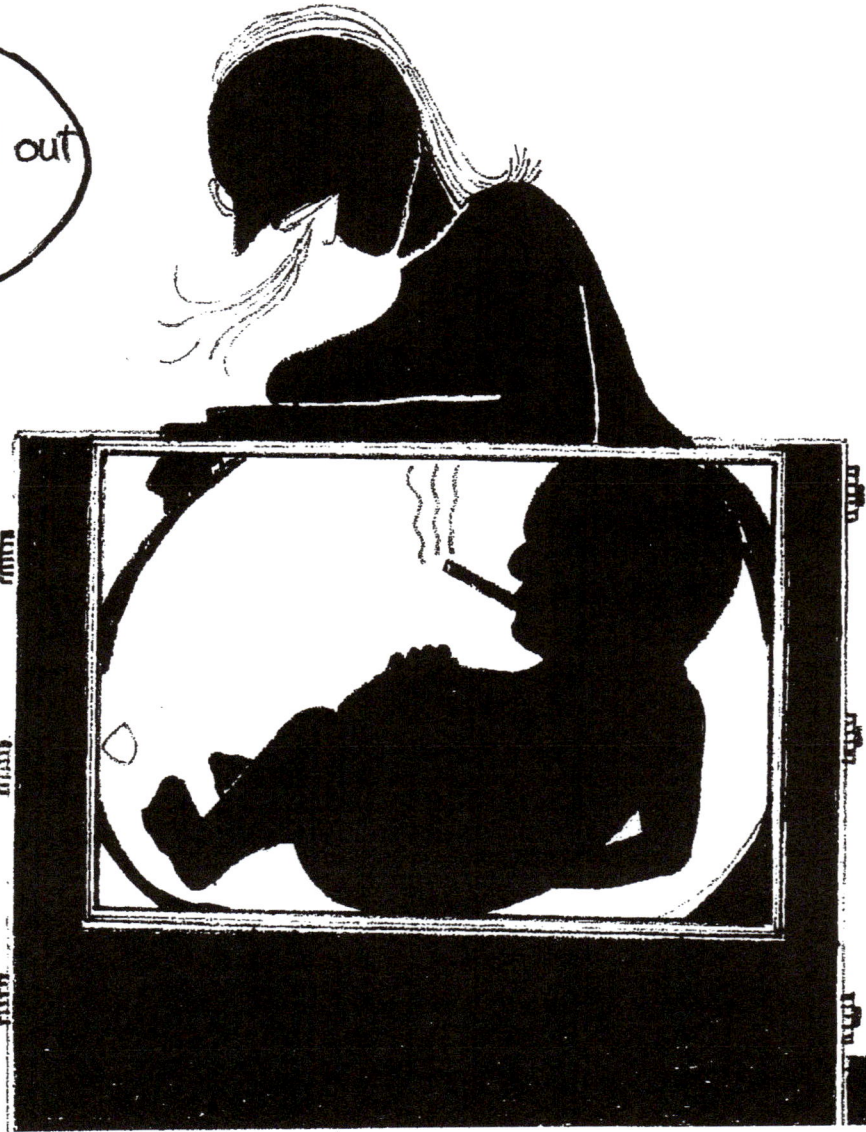

THE LAST MIRAGE
OF OUR FOSSIL FUEL CULTURE.

© DUSSEAU '08

CHEAP GAS

87 89 93

GAS

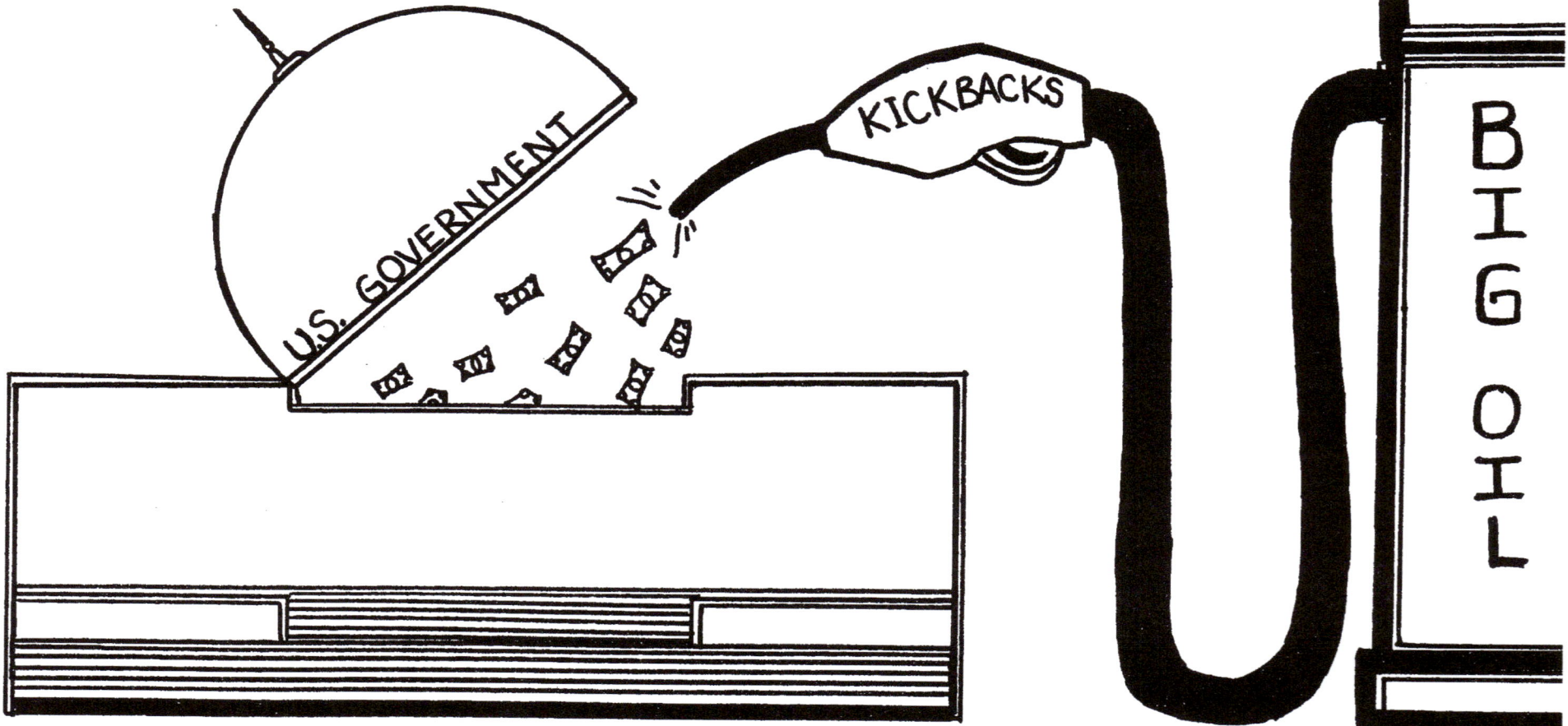

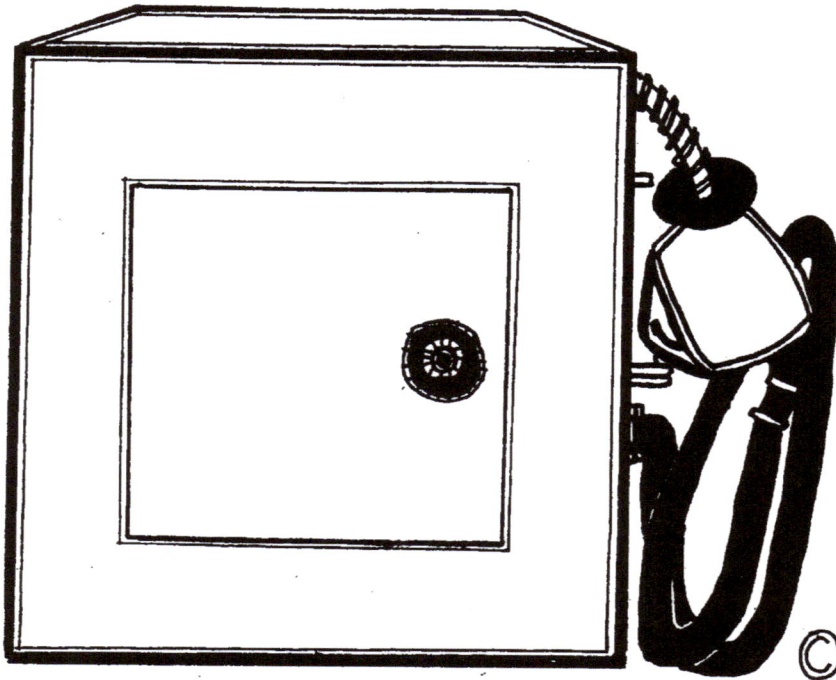

© DUSSEAU 08' 5/22/21

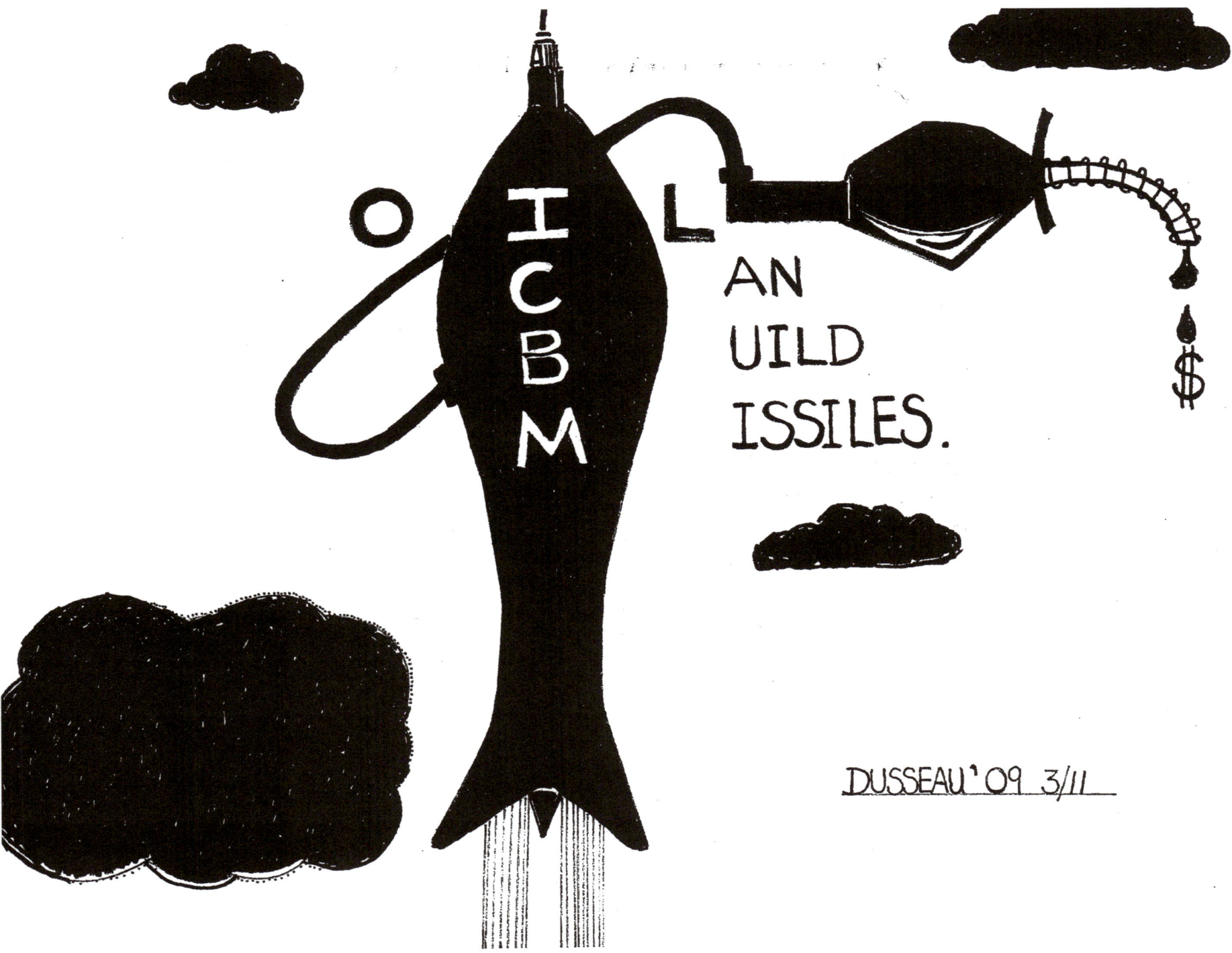

THE CHAMBERLAIN EFFECT

MORE TIME
25¢

IRANIAN APPEASEMENT

©DUSSEAU

TODAY'S SERMON:
"SPEW HATRED"
IN AMERICA!!!

PASTOR REV. WRIGHT

DUSSEAU '08 4/6

TODAY'S TOPIC: JEREMIAH WRIGHT
REVISED ETHICS 101:
SPREADING LIES ABOUT AMERICA.
(THIS IS WRONG)
USING GOD'S PULPIT TO PREACH HATE.
(THIS IS WRONG)
CONCLUSION: 2 WRONGS DO MAKE A WRIGHT!
ETHICS 101
'08 DUSSEAU 3/22

BIRTH OF THE AMERICAN CULTURE OF VIOLENCE.

CHILDREN BORN INTO THE CYCLE OF VIOLENCE.

© DUSSEAU '09 8/24/16

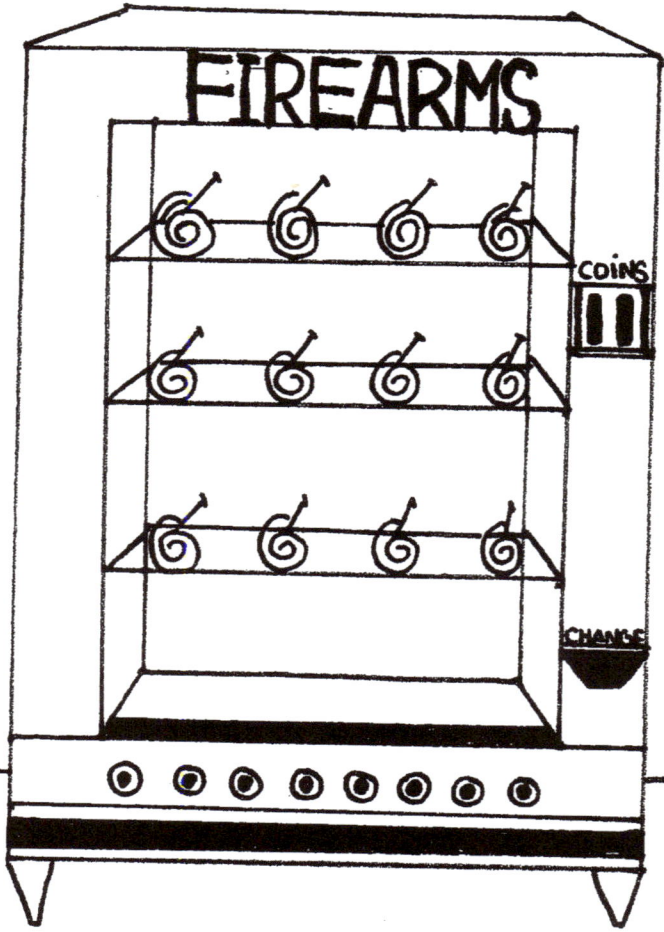

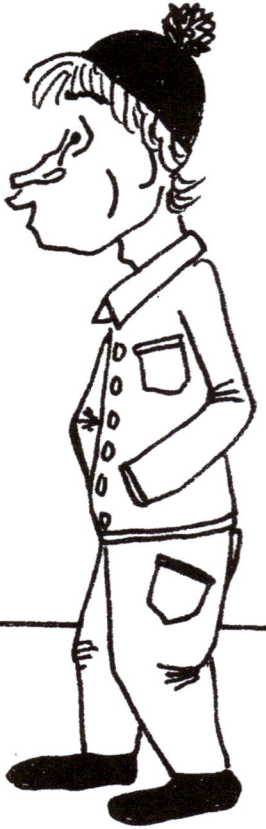

ANONYMOUS
EMPLOYEE
TIPS

© DUSSEAU '15

www.ingramcontent.com/pod-product-compliance
Lightning Source LLC
Chambersburg PA
CBHW040710150426

42811CB00061B/1812